THE ART OF

BARBIE™

The Art of Barbie

PATRICK McDONNELL
Pen & ink, watercolor, photo collage on envelope
24.8 x 21.8

THE ART OF

BARBIE™

Edited by *Craig Yoe*

WORKMAN PUBLISHING NEW YORK

Library of Congress Cataloging-in-Publication Data
The Art of Barbie™/edited by Craig Yoe
p. cm.
ISBN 1-56305-691-7
ISBN 1-56305-751-4 (paper)
1. Barbie ® dolls in art–catalogs. 2. Art, modern–20th century–catalogs.
3. Barbie ® dolls–clothing–catalogs. I. Yoe, Craig.
N8217. B356 A78 1994
704.9'496887221' 0979493–dc20
94-21803z
CIP

Workman books are available at special discounts when purchased in bulk for sales promotions as well as for fundraising or educational use. Special editions or book excerpts can also be created to specification. For details, contact the Special Sales Director at the address below.

Workman Publishing Company, Inc.
708 Broadway
New York, NY 10003

Designed and packaged by
Craig Yoe Studio
Box 212
Croton On Hudson , NY 10520

Manufactured in Italy
First Printing October 1994

10 9 8 7 6 5 4 3 2 1

Dedicated with love to Clizia Gussoni, a living doll.

Acknowledgments

The amazing thing about a project like THE ART OF BARBIE™ is that it looks so simple when it's done. But in fact many people put thousands of hours into making Barbie look good.

My deepest thanks go to all the artists who gave so generously of their talents and time to this project and its associated cause, helping children affected by AIDS. Thanks to Lifesongs for AIDS, Inc., which produced The Barbie Ball to benefit pediatric AIDS service providers and which allowed us to use some pieces from that event.

My own staff gets a great big sloppy Barbie kiss: Clizia Gussoni worked cheerfully and tirelessly moving mountains of work. Elizabeth Smith was a terrific project manager. Valuable artistic input came from June Squillace. Mary Miller of Purchase University and Bill Ronalds of St. John's University provided interns, Gregory R. Peters and Joseph Kowan. And it is safe to say that without the enthusiasm and vision of my business manager, Gene Murphy, this book would never have been realized.

I was thrilled when Peter Workman decided to publish the book. He matched us with editor Ruth Sullivan whose great strength and intelligence were time and again demonstrated. Thanks to her assistants Diane Botnick and Kathy Ryan, to art directors Eddy Hirsch and Paul Hanson for helping us arrive at creative solutions, and to Wayne Kirn and Joe Martino for being so wonderfully responsive and bringing the production values of the book to the highest level.

Meryl Friedman of Mattel Toys was an ally and supporter throughout the project. When I first approached her with my book idea, Meryl was already thinking of bringing Barbie into the world of fine art and trying to raise money for children with AIDS in honor of her brother Scott, also an art lover and collector. Other people at Mattel providing much welcomed assistance were Bob Normile, Donna Gibbs, Kathy Purcell, Cynthia Crossland, Judy Tsuno, and Lisa McKendall.

Thanks to Marvin Heiferman and Carole Kismaric of Look-Out for their expert consulting in the realm of photography, Fred Hoffman for his help enlisting fine artists, Howard Goodman for contributing his time photographing many of the works of art, and to Courtney Rosen-Hoehle for her help with the art used from the German exhibition *Kunst, Design und Barbie*.

Appreciation to George Lois, Chris Oliveros, Jay Kennedy, Craig Sheman, Jacinthe Leclerc, Lulu Johnson, Irene Cerdas, Pam Sommers, Phyllis Kind, Mayumi Kabota, Luca Boschi, Don and Maggie Thompson, Jay Kennedy, Gerald Rapp, Janine Cukierman, Lisa Silfen, and Van Toffler. As well to Katy Dobbs and Pegi Goodman of *Barbie Magazine* and Karen F. Caviale and Marlene Mura of *Barbie Bazaar* for their enthusiasm and time.

Thanks also to my good friends J.J. Sedelmaier, Alan Kaplan, Roberta Murphy, Warren Smith, J.D. King, Floriana Campanozzi, Sheryl O'Connell, and Kathy Chow who all gave help along the way. And if Janet Morra-Yoe hadn't been my best friend for over two decades, we certainly wouldn't have the artwork by our children that graces one of the first pages.

Love to Mrs. Duane Yoe, Jean Ann Bender, Giovanna Anzaldi, and Nerio Gussoni.

Foreword

I was always forced to admire Her from afar. It was 1961 and my sister and her friends would gather behind closed doors in her bedroom. Through a small crack, I'd watch as they'd open their vinyl cases and begin the almost religious rite of Playing Barbie. While they entered their fantasy land of beautiful clothes, dream houses and dream dates, I had to be content with G.I. Joe, potato guns, and Davy Crockett.

But one day, I just had to venture into my sister's room to discover for myself the forbidden treasure. My sister caught me in the act and let out a blood-curdling scream. "Mom, Craig is touching my Barbie!" And I was told in no uncertain terms, "Don't ever play with Barbie again!" My sister looked on smugly satisfied that I'd been forever barred from sacred ground.

Today, in my work as a toy inventor, I'm constantly reminded, "You're only limited by your imagination." Except, it seems, when it comes to Barbie. Mattel's designers have covered it all. Barbie has worn everything, been

everywhere, taken up every career imaginable. In other words, when brainstorming new toy ideas: Don't Play Barbie.

So I was thrilled when my book idea for THE ART OF BARBIE™ was accepted. Finally it was my turn to play with the doll. And I invited over 100 international artists to play, too. The art community was wildly enthusiastic and what's resulted is a true celebration of the original dream girl.

From Andy Warhol's celebrity silk-screen to William Wegman's sweet doll and dog tableau to Karl Lagerfeld's Barbie in a little black dress, each artist offers a fresh, surprising, sometimes provocative vision. The B-girl drew out feelings of nostalgia, flights of fantasy and telling statements about American womanhood. She inspired gentle humor, sweet romance and even near religious devotion.

Some of today's top fashion designers started out taking scraps of fabric from their mom's drawer and safety-pinning them around Barbie. Thus their enthusiasm for this project should come as no surprise.

Designers like Anna Sui, Calvin Klein, and Yves Saint Laurent deck her out in the latest fashions, while Betsey Johnson renders her in Future chic.

Barbie has to be the perfect photographers' model. She never has an extra pound or an unsightly pimple, and she can hold a pose perfectly still. Photographer David Seidner sees her through a glass darkly in "Funhouse Barbie," Sandy Skoglund has her lying and frying at the beach, and Neal Slavin constructs a diorama of Big Barbie watching little Barbies. Speaking of stunning photographers' models, Claudia Schiffer is a living doll here as The Barb.

Fine artists like Gladys Nilsson, Kenny Scharf, and Charles Burns turn the 3-D Miss B into 2-D portraits. The Muse inspired others to create life-size sculptural pieces; they give new meaning to the term "plastic arts." One minute they envision her as small as a snail and the next they make her 50 feet tall attacking Times Square. They've turned her into a motorcycle mama and a leader of a rompin' stompin' blue devil band. They've tempted her with sweets, and even pickled our plastic Mona Lisa.

Barbie's worldwide popularity is reflected in the international cast of celebrants. Artists from Italy, Germany, France, Japan, Spain, and of course, her homeland, the United States, have joined together to pay visual homage—creating clothes, friends, worlds, and personas as fresh and challenging as Barbie has ever known. There were no limits to their imagination.

So . . . I know I wasn't supposed to Play Barbie . . . but, it was every bit as exciting and fun as I had imagined. Sorry, Mom.

Craig Yoe
New York
August, 1994

Introduction

by Jill McCorkle

In the beginning, Mattel created Barbie,™ an eleven and a half inch plastic vinyl fashion queen, and they saw that this creation was more than good; it was sensational. It swept the nation, replacing babies that wet and cried with a dream goddess. The year was 1959. Hank Aaron was batting .355 and Eisenhower was in the White House. Doris Day and Rock Hudson graced the big screen in *Pillow Talk* and Sandra Dee was making her debut as Gidget. On the radio Elvis and Bobby Darin crooned about love, and everyone was reading *Lolita* and *Peyton Place*. Clearly the world was ready for a sophisticated grown-up doll, a recipient of fantasies that involved far more than motherhood.

But Barbie was lonely out there all by herself, and so in 1961 Mattel decided that she needed a companion, a soul mate, someone to go with her on that Caribbean cruise or to the Parisian fashion extravaganza. And so with a bit of flesh-colored vinyl and an extra half inch of height, they created Ken, the ever faithful "boyfriend" and ultimate Barbie acces-sory. They saw that this creation was *also* more than good and thus launched the whole Barbie society, a population that since the beginning of Barbietime has reached 800 million. Imagine the population of India clad in bubble-gum pink with free flowing synthetic hair and you begin to get the picture. There was Midge (the freckle faced girl-next-door, best friend of Barbie) and her boyfriend, Allan. There were Skipper and Skooter and Ricky and Francie, Tutti, Todd, Stacie, and Derek, who are featured here in Laura Levine's "Barbie Family Tree."

Years ago, *Mad Magazine* ran a list of gifts to give to people you didn't like and on this list (along with a Saint Bernard puppy and a five dollar gift certificate for a Cadillac) was one Barbie with no accessories; this was designed to lead your enemy into bankruptcy. As her population expanded exponentially, so did Barbie's wardrobe. You can't just have a naked Barbie (even though the first thing most children want to do to a doll is take off her clothes), and you can't very well expect her to wear the same thing to a fashion show that she wears to go ice-skating with Ken. And what about that swimsuit? I mean, sure, she almost always comes with a swimsuit, but she can't wear that same old rag season after season, and she surely can't wear it to the office! Despite popular belief, Barbie doesn't spend all of her days at the beach. Since that first striped swimsuit, more than 100 million yards of fabric have gone into making Barbie fashions that mirror her many roles. For THE ART OF BARBIE™ such top fashion designers as Yves Saint Laurent, Todd Oldham, and Karl Lagerfeld have created spectacular new styles. Barbie has had more than one billion pairs of

shoes, a fact commented on wryly here in Barbara Nessim's watercolor, "Imelda Marcos Ain't Got Nothing on Me." Barbie is trendy and she is classic; she's whatever the little hands (or big fashion designers) playing with her want her to be.

Besides reflecting our changing fashions, Barbie mirrors the expanding career choices of our times. She has gone from teenage fashion model, stewardess, graduate (1963), and candy striper to astronaut, surgeon, Olympic athlete, marine sergeant, army medic, and 1992 Presidential candidate. What's more, Barbie (who first had a Black friend, Christie, introduced in 1968) has continued to broaden her

ORIGINAL BARBIE   QUICK CURL   FIREFIGHTER   LIVE ACTION   ASTRONAUT

cultural and ethnic roots to become Italian, Japanese, Peruvian, Chinese, Native American, Russian, Kenyan, and so on.

I was born the same year as Barbie and, like most women of my generation, grew up with her. As a kid I was always in search of a brunette Barbie. My daughter at age four was obsessed with getting a Totally Hair Barbie (for the uninformed, this bestselling Barbie has hair all the way to her feet), and I was thrilled to find a brunette one. My daughter's fantasy was that she was Rapunzel after a dye job. I was once asked by a friend (a very successful businesswoman in her early fifties) if I had had Barbies growing up. "Yes," I answered cautiously, as I've often found Barbie to be a rather controversial topic. Her immediate response was "Oh, how I envy that. I loathed baby dolls and have always thought that I would have loved a real grown-up doll of independent means who could do as she pleased!" My sentiments exactly.

The more people I talk to over the years about their Barbie fantasies, the broader and more creative the possibilities. My Barbies went horseback riding (her horses have included Dancer and Dallas and Midnight and Prancer); I never owned a horse and rarely got to ride one. It was my fantasy. Ken didn't go. He belonged to my sister and stayed in his box

MARINE CORPS   DOCTOR   BARBIE FOR PRESIDENT   DAY TO NIGHT   ARMY   UPTOWN CHIC

most of the time while my Barbies rode through the wild West and my sister's Bubblecut Barbie (circa 1962) wore a black sequined evening dress—the very one featured in David Levinthal's sensuous photo "Barbie Noir"—and sang the blues.

My most memorable Barbie fantasy was one that took place with my Twist 'N Turn Barbie, for whom I saved quite a few allowances. I thought she was absolutely beautiful; she reminded me of Julie Newmar and I often dressed her up as Catwoman. I had just seen *I Want to Live*, with Susan Hayward (which I probably was not supposed to be watching), and was quite moved by all the prison scenes. My Twist 'N Turn became Susan Hayward's character and I constructed her a prison cell out of throw pillows. I sneaked my mother's electric razor, shaved her head, and put her in solitary confinement before I even thought of the consequences—a Baldheaded Barbie! For weeks I mourned the loss of my Barbie's beautiful hair, not to mention my mother's synthetically plugged up Gillette.

Apparently my Barbie prison scene is not so unusual. It so happens that the buxom fashion queen is often a creature tortured for effect. Her head pops off, fits back on, and does a 360-degree rotation. She can as readily play the role of Regan in *The Exorcist* as she can Marie Antoinette. Those who ever playacted Solitary Confinement Barbie or Salem Witch or Joan of Arc Barbie will delight in Bryon

Moore's pen-and-ink of Beavis and Butt-head playing Barbie, as well as in "Funhouse Barbie," "Pickled Barbie," and "Mummified Barbies," to name only a few wonderful explorations found in these pages.

I have in recent years found myself defending Barbie and her hot pink world to other mothers. I mean, sure, I wish her body were more realistic. I'm all in favor of Big Butt and Cellulite Barbie, but remember, Barbie is a mirror. She was not created to lead society but to follow. When fashion models begin to resemble Rubens's creations, when ample hips and thighs are in style, envied, coveted, and given the favorable body image they deserve, then I'm sure Barbie will come around. Until then, she remains high fashion's and photographers' fantasy *du jour*.

Parents who deny their children access to Barbie may find that they are seeking bigger problems than how to pick up all of those little shoes and purses at the end of a good play day. Nothing illustrates this quite as well as "Phoebe and the Pigeon People," a wonderful cartoon depicting a girl who has been given a tool set instead of the Barbie she wanted. What these artists have openly acknowledged, despite popular belief, is that there is no preordained role for Barbie, no "guide to being a bimbo" that comes with the box. Besides, who knows what all those Barbies are doing behind closed doors? Maybe they are reading Chekhov and Tolstoy while sitting in their

Jacuzzis. Maybe our Barbies are big fans of Gloria Steinem and Susan Faludi and aspire to similar heights. There are vegetarian Barbies who support Ben & Jerry and who like to take that hot pink Starlight Motor Home to Woodstock (then or now) with the Grateful Dead blasting while they eat pint after pint of Cherry Garcia and say things like "I don't worry about calories. I believe in being free and happy." I mean after all, Barbie *is* single. Sure there have been many many wedding outfits over the years and yes, Midge and Allan did get married and disappear for a while (life in suburbia? a houseful of kids? divorce? you decide), but Barbie has remained on her own.

Barbie is 35 this year, and look at all she has done! She's a pop culture icon of more than one generation and, with this book, has even surpassed her own previous level of fame. This interpretive art—the fact that Barbie was deemed worthy by the likes of Warhol—is proof of her ever-growing and changing image. Barbie *is* fashion and trend. She has joined the ranks of Marilyn and Elvis and Mickey. For the older generation she's a fad, she's camp ("Barbie Throws a Party"), sometimes nostalgic (as in "Commuter Set 1959" and "Party Line") and sometimes futuristic ("Cyber-Bride" and "Planet Pink"). She is for many artists here an image of the unattainable, the perfect woman—"Daphne," Venus, and "La Vergine"—and for others she's vampish and wild like "Biker Barbie." For many people, all Barbies look alike and the subtle distinction of various years and hairstyles are overlooked. Thus, the tribe of Stepford Barbies depicted in the hilarious "Barbie on the Beach" and "Barbie Island."

For visual parodies of art masterpieces, there are Marian Jones's "Nude Barbie Descending a Staircase" (it reminds me of our bathtub when the water drains and a heap of naked Barbies are left to drip-dry), "Analysis of Beauty" after Hogarth, and my favorite, "The Color of Evening," in which Barbie appears in Edward Hopper's "Nighthawks." And, of course, there's William Wegman's take on Barbie, his famous weimaraner humorously enthroned in a Barbie dream house. Anyone made of flesh and blood (or plastic vinyl) will love this work of creative imagination as Barbie and her pink universe are reinvented and immortalized.

Barbie

ANDY WARHOL
Synthetic polymer paint and silkscreen ink on canvas
101.6 x 101.6

Nude Barbie Descending a Staircase

MARIAN JONES
Photograph
20.3 x 25.4

Housebroken

WILLIAM WEGMAN
Unique 20" x 24" Polaroid Polacolor ER
51 x 61

Big Barbie

NEAL SLAVIN
Photograph
10.2 x 12.7

Barbluella

KENNY SCHARF
Acrylic on canvas
51 x 61

Biker Barbie

DOUGLAS FRASER
Alkyd on paper
20.7 x 33.4

Flower Child

BETSEY JOHNSON
Doll and fabric
21 x 3 x 29

Retro Shades

TRISH BURGIO
Oil
35.5 x 35.5

TODD
OLDHAM
4
"BARBIE"

Hot Chic

TODD OLDHAM
Ink on paper
29.7 x 43.1

B-girl in an A-line

D. MADELINE COATES
Oil on clayboard
45.7 x 60.9

Beauty and the Beast

PETER ENGELHARDT
Papier-mâché figure and doll
152.4 x 152.4 x 213.4

Barbie in a Lagerfeld Straindress

Karl Lagerfeld 94

*L*ittle *B*lack *D*ress

KARL LAGERFELD
Pastel
29.5 x 42

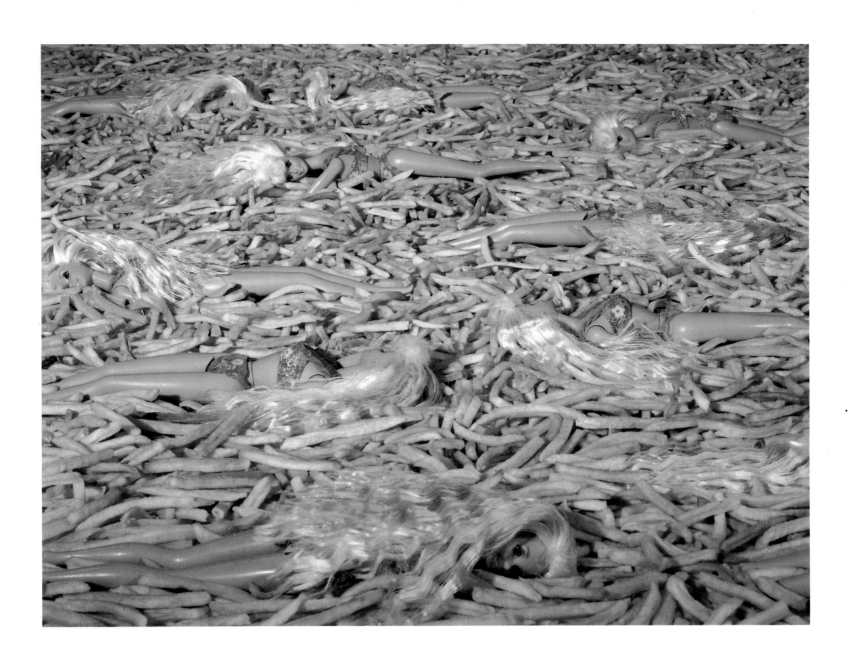

Barbie at the Beach

SANDY SKOGLUND
Color photograph
25.4 x 20.3

. 3   0

Funhouse Barbie

DAVID SEIDNER
Silver print
28 x 36

Girlie

FIONA SMYTH
Gouache
20.5 x 25.5

Rooftop Romance

STEVE DININNO
Acrylic on paper
23.2 x 19.7

The Kiss

HOLGER SCHEIBE
Color photograph and antique wood frame
61 x 3.8 x 91.4

Sweater Girl 1959

SHEILA METZNER
Transparency on fresson print
33 x 48.3

Barbie's Elvis Sighting

CHARLES BURNS
Film positive, paper, acrylic paint
16.8 x 27

3 6

Prehistoric Traces

QUENBY CHUNKO
Pastel
35.5 x 31

The Bride Wore Red

YVES SAINT LAURENT (dress)
FRANCESCO SCAVULLO (photo)
Alexandre Zouari (hair)
Dress: tulle and tulle point d'esprit red
Color photograph
21 x 3 x 29

Barbie in Beatsville

J.D. KING
Pen & ink with color film
24 x 24

Barbie Noir

DAVID LEVINTHAL
Polaroid Polacolor ER print
50 x 60

Barbie Buys a Hat

GLADYS NILSSON
Watercolor
29.2 x 38.3

Imelda Marcos Ain't Got Nothing on Me

BARBARA NESSIM
Watercolor and ink
23.6 x 28.3

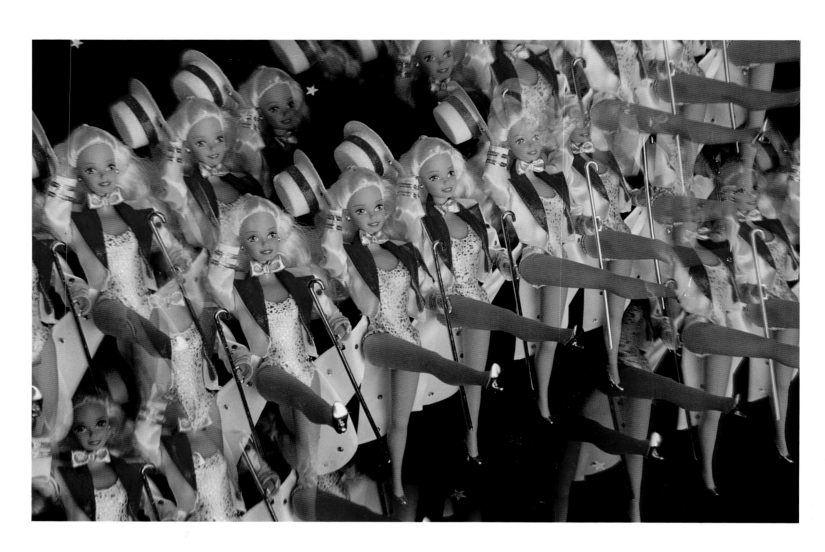

Sixty-six Kicks

BARRY STURGILL
Color transparency
35 mm

Icon

CAROL PELIGIAN
Mixed media
812 x 1016

Party Line

MITCH O'CONNELL
Watercolor
99 x 129

La Bambolona

GUIDO CREPAX

Ink

15 x 21

Barbie and What's His Name Get Married

HIRO YAMAGATA
Photograph
12.2 x 15.3

And They Lived Happily Ever After

HARTMUT TROMBEREND
and HANS-OTTO BATHEN
Mixed media
122 x 91.4 x 152.4

The Temptations of Barbie

DAVID GOLDIN
Mixed media and a Barbie doll
68 x 97

𝓑arbie Family Tree

LAURA LEVINE
Acrylic on masonite
58 x 47

What will I wear?

The In Crowd

Mood Music

"I Got You, Babe"

Barbie Throws a Party

KENI VALENTI
Polaroids
10.2 X 10.3

"Far out!"

"Dance Fever"

Ice breaker

Party hearty

Hear Me Roar

SARA SCHWARTZ
Clay
45.7 x 45.7

Analysis of Beauty (After Hogarth)

JOHN CRAIG
Collage
32.5 x 28.9

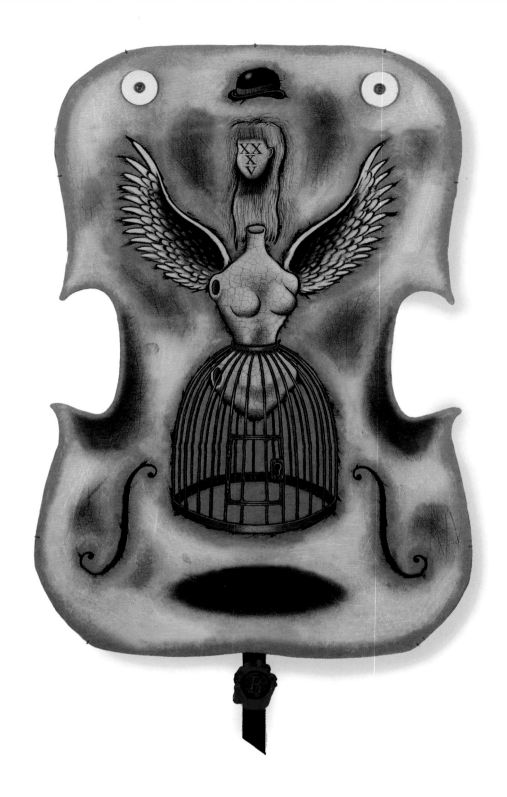

XXXV

POL TURGEON
Mixed media
30 x 44

Peace-Barbie

ANDREAS WEBER
Mixed media
65 x 55 x 50.8

Dream Girl

MEL ODOM
Oil
35.5 x 45.7

Planet Pink
or Barbie in the Sky with Glasses

CRAIG YOE
Mixed media
45 x 60

Barbie Island

BRIAN SHERIDAN
Photo composite
35.7 x 25.8

Valley of the Doll

RAOUL VITALE
Oil on masonite
32.4 x 40.7

Water Barbie

MILO MANARA
Pen, ink and watercolor
10.2 x 12.7

Attack of the 50-Foot Barbie

JILL GREENBERG
Photograph - digital manipulation
17.2 x 27.4

Pop Barbie

DAVID H. COWLES
Gouache
17.5 x 28.5

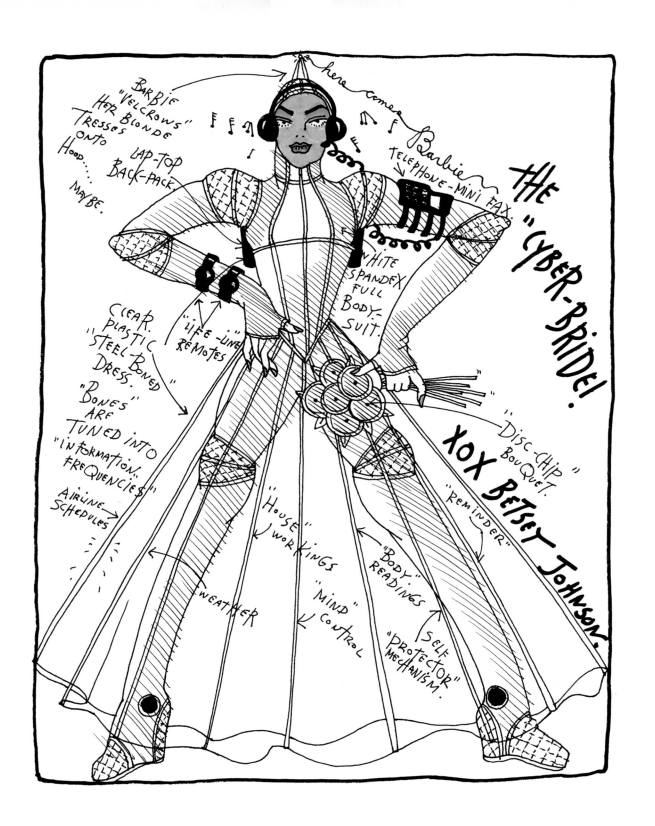

Cyber-Bride

BETSEY JOHNSON
Marker and pencil on paper
21 x 28.5

Bugs Barbie

CHUCK JONES
Original animation cel
30.5 x 26.6

Huh Huh Huh. Cool! Yeah. Heh Heh.

BRYON MOORE
Pen & ink
18 x 15

Heavy Metal Barbie

SEYMOUR CHWAST
Acrylic on sheet metal
100 x 65

Big Hair Barbie

ALISON SEIFFER
Gouache
14 x 26.5

Taxi Dancers

KEN BOTTO
Ektacolor print
50 x 60

Monster Truck Barbie

FLOWER FRANKENSTEIN
& BRUCE HILVITZ
Serigraph on paper and cloth
9 x 26 x 33

Guess Who's Coming for Sushi

BARRY STURGILL
Color slide
35 mm

Kid Kong

CLIZIA GUSSONI
Pastel
26 x 25

Photo: Kelly O'Connor

Put Another Shrimp on the Barbie, Mate

RICK THARP
Shrimp and doll
29 x 5.5 x 21

Barbie with Handy Horse

ALAN E. COBER
Ink, prismacolor
42 x 30

Museum Piece

ISABEL HAMM
Clay
45.7 x 61

Cubist Barbie

GEORGANNE DEEN
Collage
21.5 x 30.5

Star Trekking

PETER BERMES
Doll, propeller, rotation device and plastic
91.4 x 7.6 x 76.2

Birth of Barbie

EMILY COHEN
Pastel and colored pencil
45 x 39

Barbie Scream

ADAM NIKLEWICZ
Acrylic
15 x 20

The Color of the Evening

NERIO GUSSONI
Computer
24 x 18

Horizontal and Vertical Barbies (Color-Coded)

JOHN BALDESSARI
Black & white photographs, color photographs, colored stickers
20 x 18

Flat Top
MARLIES MÖLLER
Doll, hair spray, glue and gray hair dye
21 x 3 x 29

Deco Doll

TIM LEWIS
Watercolor
21.2 x 26.2

1-2-3 Barbie!

IRENE ROFHEART PIGOTT
Oil, acrylic and flashe
38 x 45.5

Barbiestock

JORDI LABANDA
Watercolor
42 x 59.4

Love My Tender

ANNE JUD
& HERBERT JAKOB WEINAND
Dolls, U.S. dollar bills and bottle
40 x 5 x 40

Take Another Turn on the Catwalk, Barbie

From left : AMY CHAN, CAROLINA HERRERA, CHROME HEARTS,
NICOLE MILLER, CALVIN KLEIN, LIZ CLAIBORNE

Littlest Angel

REVEREND HOWARD FINSTER
Paint on Barbie doll
21 x 3 x 29

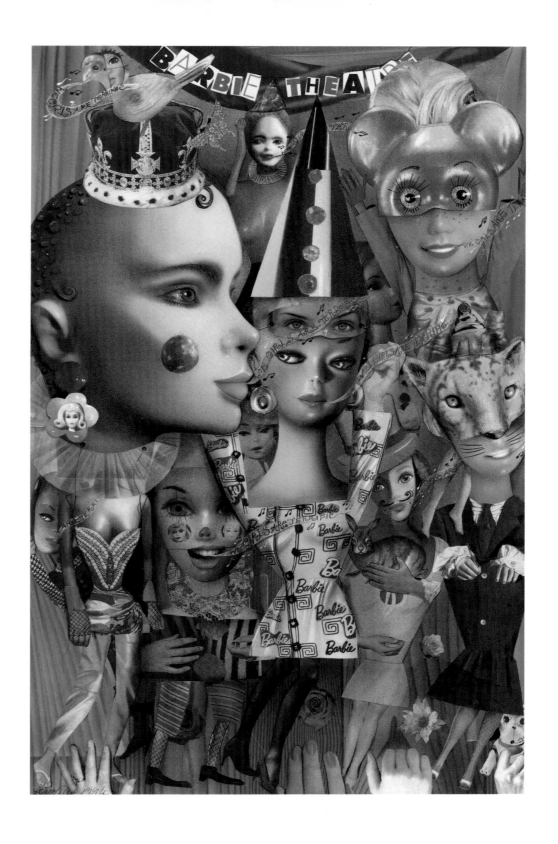

We Girls Are Terrific

JANET WOOLLEY
Montage and acrylic
45 x 60

Twinkle Belle

ROBERT FINK
Chandelier, cut glass and dolls
65 x 65 x 110

Altar of Love

JÖRG WYROWSKI
Paint, styrofoam, Barbie Jaguar and dolls
61 x 10.2 x 50.8

Phoebe and the Pigeon People

JAY LYNCH
& GARY WHITNEY
Pen & ink
412 x 133

Hatched

LISA MANNING
Airbrush acrylic
30 x 50

Queen of Hearts
and Gold Mackie

BOB MACKIE
Marker and pencil (left)
Vinyl doll and material (right)
10.1 x 12.7 and 21 x 3 x 29

Neptune Fantasy Barbie

BOB MACKIE
Vinyl doll and material
21 x 3 x 29

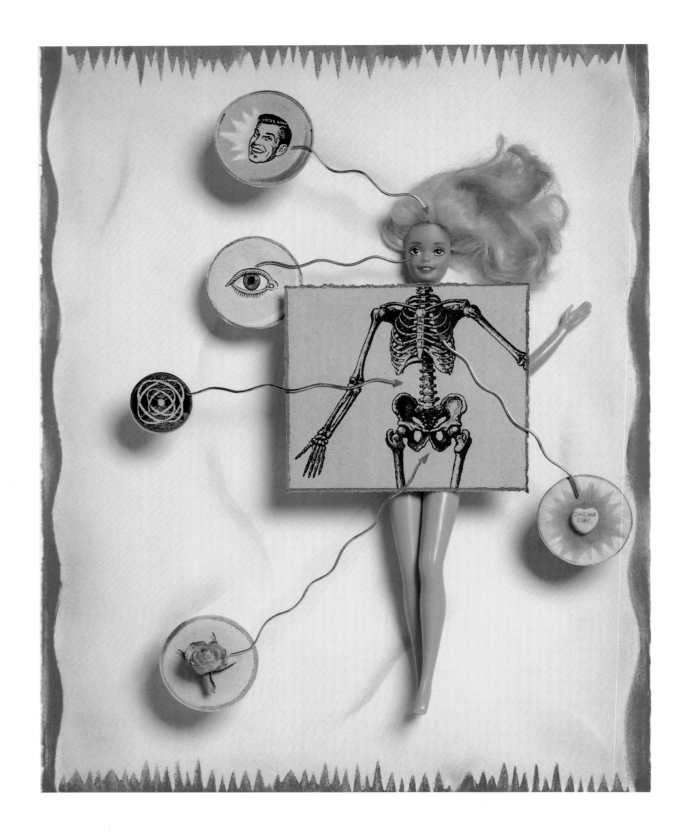

X - Ray

MARY ANN SMITH
Collage and pastel
24 x 30

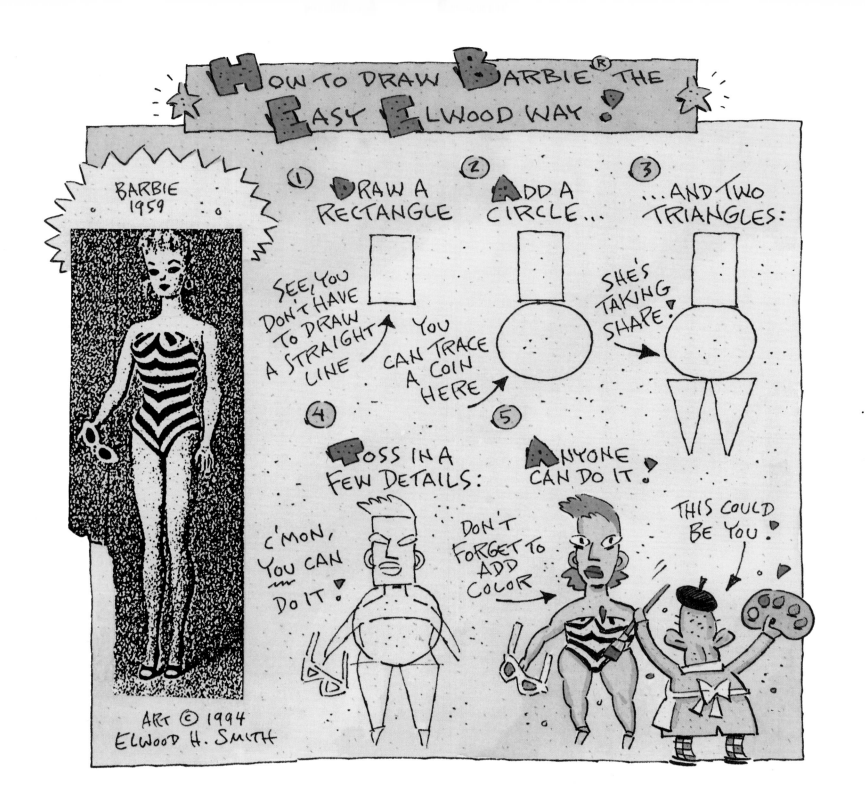

Draw This Doll

ELWOOD H. SMITH
Watercolor and India ink
18.4 x 18.4

9 8

Where Is She Now?

KEN BOTTO
Ektacolor print
50 X 60

Wanna-B

CLAUDIA SCHIFFER
Photograph by Gilles Bensimon
Live model
5'11"

→BARBIE'S·ROMPIN'·STOMPIN'·ALL·STAR·BLUE DEVIL BAND··

Jazzed

JAMES FLORA
Acrylic
44 x 31

Pas de Deux

LOIS GREENFIELD
Gelatin - silver
18 x 18

Midge Mattel and Her Barbies
Philadelphia, PA

DAVID GRAHAM
Dye coupler photograph
48.3 x 48.3

Oh! Barbie!!!

GEORGANNE DEEN
Computer/ink jet collage
26 x 39.5

But Enough About Me

TOM GARRETT
Collage
39 x 39

Barbie in Wonderland

LAUREN URAM
Paper
30.9 x 22.5

COMMUTER SET
1 9 5 9

Commuter Set 1959

ISAAC MIZRAHI
Gouache
23 x 30.5

Belle on Wheels

RITASUE SIEGEL
Photo collage
50 x 54

La Barbie Vergine

JOEL PETER JOHNSON
Oil on board
13.8 x 19.5

All That Glitters

FREDERICK'S OF HOLLYWOOD
Doll and fabric
21 x 3 x 29

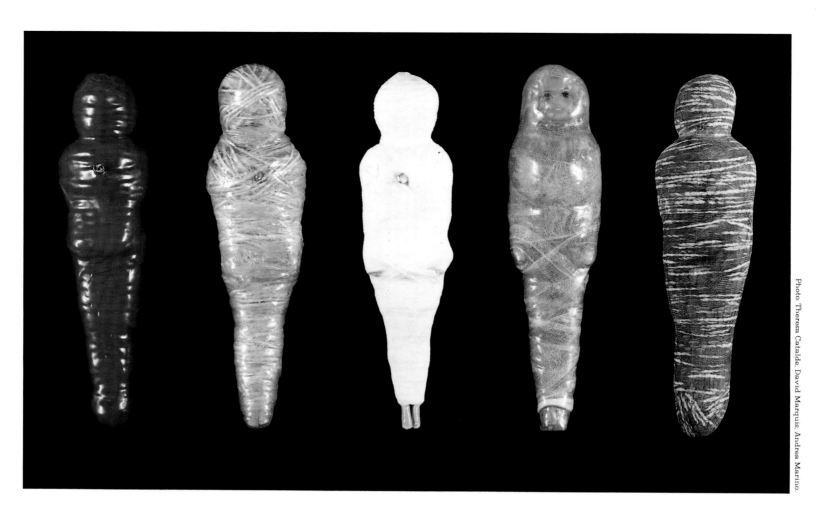

Photo: Theresa Cataldo, David Marquis, Andrea Marino.

Mummified Barbies

E.V. DAY
Mixed media and a Barbie doll
9 x 5 x 31 each piece

Pickled Barbie

FRANK LINDOW
Jar, food stuff and doll
10 x 10 x 29

1 1 2

Downtown Barbie and Ken

JEAN PHILIPPE DELHOMME
Gouache
13.5 x 24

Boot Up

ANNA SUI
Doll and fabric
21 x 3 x 29

Good Hair Day

VIDAL SASSOON
Dolls, hair spray and gel
21 x 3 x 29

Photo: Alice McCabe.

Daphne Barbie

MEL ODOM
Mixed media
38.1 x 30.5 x 25.4

Stand by Your Man

CHRIS CALLIS
Photograph
6 x 6

The Last Time I Saw Barbie

SUSAN ROSE
Mixed media
24.1 x 26.7

Kiss Kiss

JOHN BALDESSARI
Color print and rubber stamp
19 x 24

Index of Artists

The type for THE ART OF BARBIE is Commercial Script and Parade Script.
Color separations, printing and binding provided by Arnoldo Mondadori Editore, Verona, Italy.
The paper is 100# R400 Matte Satin.
The dimensions for the art are in centimeters and are approximate.